KIDDERMINSTER

BEWDLEY · STOURPORT-ON-SEVERN

CW00344956

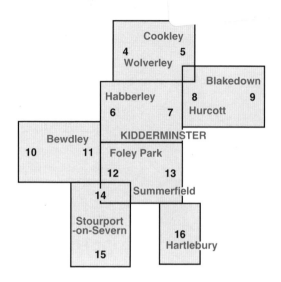

Cookley
4   5
Wolverley

Blakedown
8   9
Habberley
6   7   Hurcott

KIDDERMINSTER
Bewdley
10   11   Foley Park
12   13

14   Summerfield

Stourport
-on-Severn
16
Hartlebury
15

Every effort has been made to verify
the accuracy of information in this
book but the publishers cannot accept
responsibility for expense or loss
caused by an error or omission.
Information that will be of assistance
to the user of the maps will be welcomed.

The representation on these maps of a
road, track or path is no evidence of the
existence of a right of way.

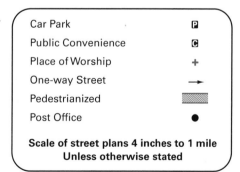

Car Park	🅿
Public Convenience	🅲
Place of Worship	+
One-way Street	→
Pedestrianized	▨
Post Office	●

Scale of street plans 4 inches to 1 mile
Unless otherwise stated

Street plans prepared and published by ESTATE PUBLICATIONS, Bridewell House,
TENTERDEN, KENT, and based upon the ORDNANCE SURVEY mapping with the permission
of The Controller of H. M. Stationery Office.

The Publishers acknowledge the co-operation of the local authorities
of towns represented in this atlas.

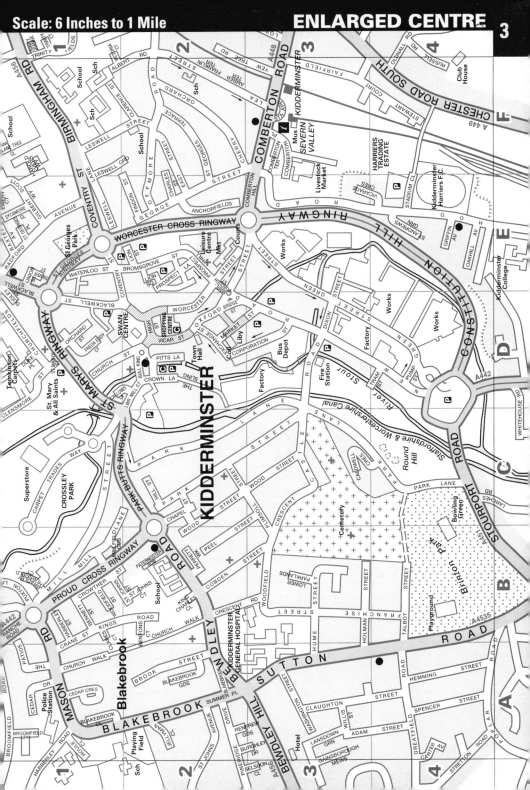

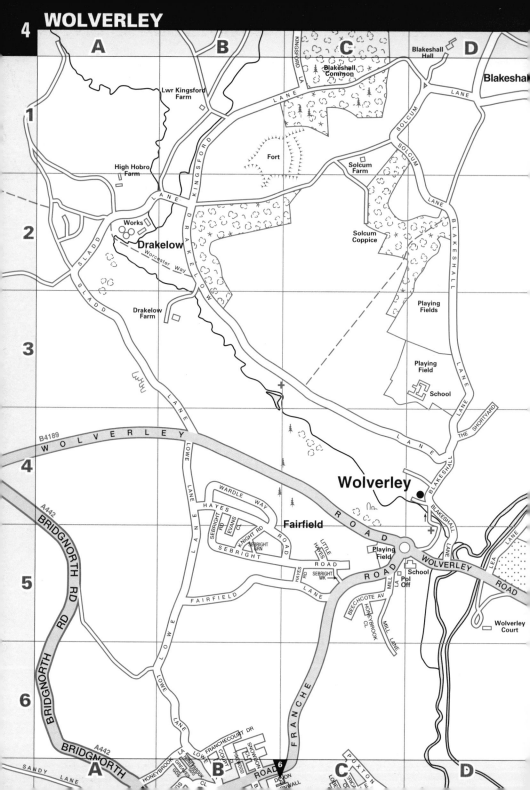

KIDDERMINSTER

Broadwaters

Greenhill

Comberton

Sports Ground

Stack Pool

Playing Field

Podmore Pool

IND EST

TRADING CENTRE

Factory

GREEENHILL IND EST

Council Offices

Cricket Ground

CROSSLEY PARK

St Georges Park

COVENTRY ST

School

Swan Centre

Market Cts

Leisure Cen

Bus Depot

Fire Sta

Works

Round Hill

KIDDERMINSTER SEVERN VALLEY

Market

HARRIERS TRADING ESTATE

Kidderminster Harriers F C

Club House

Schools

College

Staffordshire & Worcestershire Canal

River Stour

Playing Field

THE ROSE THEATRE

Pol Sta

Pol Office

School

School

School

School

School

A **B** **C** **D**

Chamberline Wood

Dowles

Dowles Farm

Town Coppice

RIVER SEVERN

Caravan Site

1

W Y R E

Hitterhill Coppice

DRY MILL LANE

FOREST

The Lakes

WOODTHORPE DRIVE

2

TANNERS

LANE

DRY MILL LANE

CLEOBURY ROAD

Bark Hill

WINBROOK

3

Beaucastle

Caravan Park

HILL ROAD

WYRE ROAD

School

PARK LANE

HIGHCLERE

4

A456 LONGBANK

CLEOBURY

B4190

BEWDLEY

BY-PASS

Park Dingle

Long Bank

Club House

Golf Course

Park Farm

Snuffmill Dingle

ROAD

5

Rock Coppice

HEIGHTINGTON

Ribbesford Wood

6

Park End

School

A **B** **C** **D**

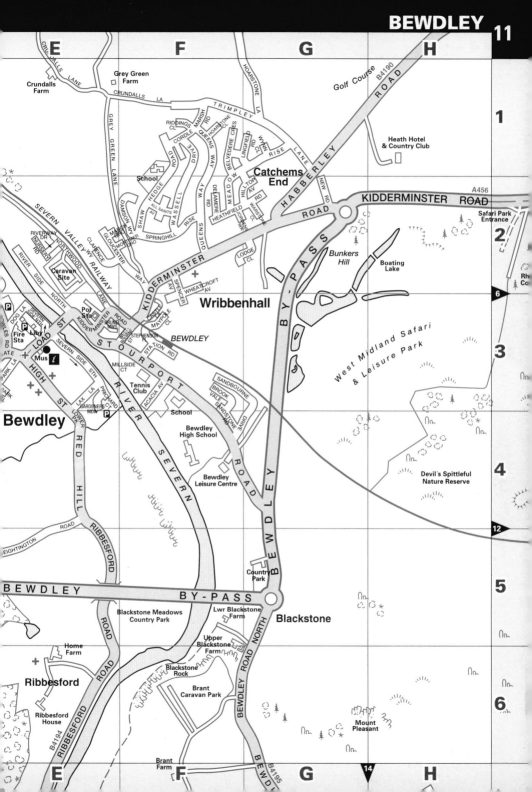

Map grid references: E, F, G, H (columns) and 1, 2, 3, 4, 5, 6 (rows)

Crundalls Farm
CRUNDALLS LANE
Grey Green Farm
Grey Green Lane
CRUNDALLS LA
Golf Course
B4190 ROAD
RIDDINGS CL
CORDLE MARSH RD
QUEENS WAY
TRIMPLEY LANE
HOARSTONE LA
LINGFIELD
BELVEDERE CRES
WYRE RISE
HILL TOP
Catchems End
Heath Hotel & Country Club
School
MEADOW RD
DELAMERE RD
HEATHFIELD RD
WARSTONE RD
LOTHIER CL
HABBERLEY ROAD
NEW RD
A456
KIDDERMINSTER ROAD
Safari Park Entrance
SHAW HEDGE
ALL SAINTS RD
DAMSON WY
SPRINGHILL
QUEENS RD
GLOUCESTER
MORTIMER RD
RISE
LODGE CL
RIVERWAY
NORTHWOOD
RIVER RD
CLARENCE
KIDDERMINSTER WAY
SPENCER
WHEATCROFT AV
MAYPOLE CL
Bunkers Hill
Boating Lake
West Midland Safari & Leisure Park
Rh Co
SEVERN VALLEY RAILWAY
Caravan Site
RIVER SIDE NORTH
LANE
Wribbenhall
BY-PASS ROAD
2
6
3
DOG LA
BRIDGE RD
Pol Sta
BRUNEL MWS
STEPHENSON
BEWDLEY
STATION RD
MILLSIDE CT
Tennis Club
PRICHARD
ACACIA AV
SANDSTONE DRIVE
SANDBOURNE
BROOK VALE
School
Devil's Spittleful Nature Reserve
Fire Sta
Liby
LOAD ST
Mus
HIGH ST
SEVERN SIDE STH
GARDENERS MDW
Bewdley High School
Bewdley Leisure Centre
BEWDLEY ROAD
12
Bewdley
RED HILL
RIVER SEVERN
STOURPORT ROAD
4
EIGHTINGTON
RIBBESFORD
BEWDLEY ROAD NORTH
Country Park
BEWDLEY BY-PASS
Blackstone
5
Blackstone Meadows Country Park
Lwr Blackstone Farm
Upper Blackstone Farm
Home Farm
RIBBESFORD ROAD
Blackstone Rock
Brant Caravan Park
Mount Pleasant
Ribbesford
Ribbesford House
B4194 RIBBESFORD ROAD
Brant Farm
BEWDLEY
B4195
14
6

E   F   G   H

Grid references: A, B, C, D across the top and bottom; 1, 2, 3, 4, 5, 6 down the sides.

Named places:
- Rhydd Covert
- Whitehill Wood
- Devils Spittleful
- Gorse Covert
- Rifle Range Nature Reserve
- Schools
- Birchen Coppice
- Burlish Camp
- Foley Park
- Amb Sta
- Beauchamp
- Sugar Beet Factory
- Vale Industrial Estate
- Sewage Works
- Oldington Trading Estate
- Trading Estate
- Foley Business Park
- Works
- Coppice Heights
- St Patricks
- Meredith Green
- Sports Ground
- Firs Industrial Estate
- Burlish Park
- Refuse Tip
- Wilden Pool
- Wilden
- Wilden Ind Est
- Staffordshire & Worcestershire Canal
- Rec Grd
- Playing Field
- Sch
- Reservoir

Roads and streets:
- Sutton Park
- Hazel
- Perrin
- Tomkinson Drive
- Tomkinson
- Lister
- Hamilton Rd
- Parry Rd
- Brinton Cl
- Woodward
- Brinton
- Connaught
- Poplar Road
- The Serpentine
- Larches Cott Gdns
- Northumberland Av
- Neville Av
- Neville Ct
- Blount Ter
- Beauchamp Ct
- Lisle Avenue
- Stourport Road
- Whitehill
- Whitegate Dr
- Sutton Rise
- Naylor
- Rifle Range
- Vera Roberts Way
- Spring Grove Cres
- Godson Cres
- Godson Pl
- Summer Road
- Goldthorn Rd
- Elmley Cl
- Teme Av
- Severn Rd
- Dowles Rd
- Arley Cl
- Dowles Cl
- Witley Cl
- Jubilee Drive North
- Victoria Rd
- Goldthorn Road
- Foley Rd
- Woodbury Road
- Jubilee Drive South
- Nash Farm Rd
- Corndon Cl
- Wrekin Road
- Walton
- Cotswold Cl
- Clee Av
- Gould Avenue East
- Gould Avenue West
- Ferguson Dr
- Addersbrooke Cres
- Walter Nash Rd East
- Whittall Dr
- Clent Av
- Whittall Drive East
- Malvern Vw
- Tolley Rd
- Bredon Rd
- Clifton Rd
- Blackford Cl
- Kinver Nash Way
- Walter Croft
- Kinver Av
- Walter Nash Road West
- Oldington Lane
- Ricketts Cl
- Parker Pl
- Kingsway
- Buttermere Rd
- Ullswater Av
- Coniston
- Ennerdale Rd
- Burlish Cl
- Windermere
- Bigbury
- The Slad
- Minster Road (B4451 / A451)

Marker numbers: 6, 11, 14

Stourport-on-Severn

Lower Heath

Hartlebury Common

Nature Reserve

SANDY LANE INDUSTRIAL ESTATE

Works

WORCESTER ROAD

A4025

River Stour

SEVERN

River Stour

MITTON

Caravan Site

Caravan Park

Marina

Weir

Redstone Rock

The Walshes

Astley Cross

Sports Ground

Swimming Pool

Sports Centre

Caravan Site

Areley Hall

Areley Kings

Coneygreen Farm

Burnthorn Brook

DUNLEY RD

DUNLEY RD

COMMON

ARELEY COMMON

B4196

B4194

PEARL LA

RIBBESFORD ROAD

A451

Rec Grd

Redstone Rock

Pol Sta

Windmill CL

School

Oakhampton Road

The Index includes some names for which there is insufficient space on the maps. These names are preceded by an * and are followed by the nearest adjoining thoroughfare.

BEWDLEY

Acacia Av DY12	11 F3
All Saints Av DY12	11 F2
Baldwin Rd DY12	10 C2
Bark Hill DY12	10 D3
Barratts Cl DY12	10 D3
Barratts Stile La DY12	10 D3
Belvedere Cres DY12	11 F1
Bewdley By-Pass	10 B5
Bewdley Rd North DY12	11 F6
Birch Tree Rd DY12	10 D4
Bramley Way DY12	10 C3
Branches Cl DY12	10 C4
Brook Vale DY12	11 F3
Brunel Mews DY12	11 E3
Castle La DY12	11 F3
Cherry Cl DY12	10 C4
Church Vw DY12	10 D3
Clarence Way DY12	11 E2
Cleobury Rd DY12	10 B4
Cobham Cres DY12	10 D3
Coniston Way DY12	10 C3
Cordle Marsh Rd DY12	11 F1
Crundalls La DY12	11 E1
Damson Way DY12	11 F2
Delamere Rd DY12	11 F2
Derwent Dr DY12	10 C2
Dog La DY12	11 E3
Dowles Rd DY12	10 C1
Dry Mill La DY12	10 B1
Early River Pl DY12	10 C3
Elan Cl DY12	10 C3
Ellesmere Dr DY12	10 C3
Elton Rd DY12	10 C3
Forest Cl DY12	10 D3
Fort Mahon Pl DY12	10 D3
Gardeners Mdw DY12	11 E3
Gloucester Way DY12	11 E2
Greenbank Rd DY12	10 C4
Grey Green La DY12	11 E1
Grosvenor Wood DY12	10 C3
Habberley Rd DY12	11 G2
Hales Pk DY12	10 C3
Hawthorn Cres DY12	10 B4
Heathfield Rd DY12	11 F2
Heightington Rd DY12	10 C6
Hernes Nest DY12	10 D4
High St DY12	11 E3
Highclere DY12	10 D4
Highclere Dr DY12	10 D4
Hilltop Av DY12	11 G2
Hoarstone Cl DY12	11 F1
Hoarstone La DY12	11 G1
Hop Pole La DY12	11 F1
Hornbeam Cl DY12	10 C4
Hornbeam Ho DY12	10 C3
Ingram Cres DY12	10 D2
Ironside Cl DY12	10 C4
Jordens Walk DY12	11 F2
Kidderminster Rd DY12	11 E3
Lakes Ct DY12	10 C3
Lambourne Dr DY12	10 C2
Lancaster Rd DY12	10 D3
Lax La DY12	11 E3
Laxton Dr DY12	10 C3
Lingfield Rd DY12	11 G1
*Little Grange Cotts, Cleobury Rd DY12	10 C2
Load St DY12	11 E3
Lodge Cl DY12	11 F2
Longbank DY12	10 A5
Lower Pk DY12	11 E4
Lyttleton Rd DY12	10 D3
March Gro DY12	11 E2
Maypole Cl DY12	11 F3
Meadow Rise DY12	11 F2
Merricks Cl DY12	10 C3
Merricks La DY12	10 C3
Millside Ct DY12	11 E3
Morella Cl DY12	11 F2
Mortimer Gro DY12	11 F2
Muskoka DY12	10 C3
New Rd DY12	11 G2
Newton Cl DY12	10 C2
Northwood La DY12	11 E2
Nursery Rd DY12	11 E2
Oakwood Rd DY12	10 D3
Orchard Rise DY12	10 D3
Park Cl DY12	11 E3
Park Dingle DY12	10 B4
Park La DY12	10 C4
Patchetts La DY12	10 D3
*Pewterers Alley, Kidderminster Rd DY12	11 E3
Pinetree Rd DY12	10 C4
Prichard Cl DY12	11 E3
Queens Way DY12	11 F1
Red Hill DY12	11 E4
Ribbesford Rd DY12	11 E6
Richmond Rd DY12	10 C3
Riddings Cl DY12	11 F1
River Side North DY12	11 E2
Riverway Dr DY12	11 E2
Rosenhurst Dr DY12	10 D3
Russett Way DY12	10 C2
Sabrina Dr DY12	10 D2
Sandbourne Dr DY12	11 F3
Sandstone Rd DY12	11 F4
Sandy Bank DY12	11 E3
Severn Side North DY12	11 E3
Severn Side South DY12	11 E3
Severn Way DY12	10 C4
Shaw Hedge Rd DY12	11 F2
Snuff Mill Walk DY12	10 D4
Spencer Av DY12	11 F2
Springhill Rise DY12	11 F3
Station Rd DY12	11 F3
Stephenson Pl DY12	11 F3
Stourport Rd DY12	11 E3
Tanners Hill DY12	10 A3
Telford Dr DY12	10 D3
The Lakes Rd DY12	10 C3
The Orchard DY12	10 C3
The Racks DY12	10 D3
Trimpley La DY12	11 F1
Tudor Rd DY12	10 C3
Valley Vw DY12	10 C4
Venus Bank DY12	10 D3
Warstone Cl DY12	11 G2
Wassell Dr DY12	11 F2
Waterloo Rd DY12	10 C3
Welch Gate DY12	10 D3
Westbourne St DY12	11 F3
Wheatcroft Av DY12	11 F2
White Heart Cl DY12	10 C3
Winbrook DY12	10 D3
Woodthorpe Dr DY12	10 D2
Wynn Cl DY12	11 G1
Wyre Hill DY12	10 C4
Yew Tree Cl DY12	10 C3
Yew Tree La DY12	10 C3
York Rd DY12	10 C3

KIDDERMINSTER

Abbey Rd DY11	6 B4
Adam St DY11	3 A3
Adams Ct DY10	7 H3
Addenbrooke Cres DY11	12 B3
Aggborough Cres DY10	13 E1
Aintree Cl DY11	6 D2
Albany Cl DY10	7 H4
Albert Rd DY11	3 F1
Aldermere Rd DY11	6 D2
Almond Av DY11	6 B2
Amber Ter DY10	3 F2
Amblecote Rd DY10	7 H5
Anchorfields DY10	3 E2
Apple Tree Cl DY10	7 H2
Arley Cl DY11	12 B2
Arthur Dr DY11	13 F4
Ash Gro DY11	6 B3
Ashdene Cl, Hartlebury DY11	16 A4
Ashdene Cl, Kidderminster DY10	8 A6
Ashley Rd DY10	7 H1
Aster Av DY11	6 D1
Audley Dr DY11	6 B3
Austcliffe La DY11	5 F2
Avill Gro DY11	6 D3
Avocet Dr DY11	13 H3
Avon Rd DY11	12 C2
Axborough La DY10	5 H3
Badland Av DY10	7 F1
Baldwin Rd DY10	7 H2
Balmoral Ct DY10	7 G5
Barn Owl Pl DY10	13 G3
Barnetts Cl DY10	7 H6
Barnetts Gro DY10	7 H6
Barnetts La DY10	7 G6
Barrett Cl DY10	7 H4
Barrie Av DY10	8 A4
Baskerville Rd DY10	7 G1
Batham Rd DY10	7 G2
Baxter Av DY10	3 E1
Baxter Gdns DY10	7 F3
Beauchamp Av DY11	12 D1
Beauchamp Ct DY11	12 D2
Beaufort Av DY11	6 B3
Beaulieu Cl DY11	6 D2
Beechcote Av DY11	4 C5
Beechcroft Rd DY11	6 B2
Beeches Rd DY11	6 C1
Beechfield Dr DY11	6 C2
Beeston Rd DY10	5 G3
Belbroughton Rd DY10	9 F2
Belle Orchard DY11	6 B6
Belvedere Cl DY10	7 H5
Bennett St DY11	3 B1
Bentons Ct DY11	3 A2
Bernie Crossland Walk DY10	13 F1
Berrow Hill Rd DY11	6 B1
Beverley Cl DY11	6 A4
Bewdley Hill DY11	6 A6
Bewdley Rd DY11	3 A2
Bigbury La DY13	12 D6
Birchfield Rd DY11	6 C5
Birchwood Cl DY11	6 A3
Birmingham Rd DY10	3 F1
Biset Av DY10	7 H5
Bittern Wood Rd DY10	13 H2
Blackford Cl DY11	12 B4
Blackwell St DY10	3 D1
Blakebrook DY11	3 A1
Blakebrook Cl DY11	3 A1
Blakebrook Gdns DY11	3 A2
Blakeshall La DY11	4 D2
Blount Ter DY11	12 D1
Booton Cl DY11	7 G1
Borrington Rd DY10	7 H6
Brabham Cl DY11	7 E1
Bradley Thursfield Ct DY11	3 B1
Brambling Rise DY10	13 H3
Brampton Cl DY10	5 G4
Brecknell Rise DY10	7 F2
Bredon Rd DY11	12 B3
Brett Young Cl DY10	8 A6
Bridge Rd DY10	5 F2
Bridge St DY10	3 D2
Bridgnorth Rd DY11	4 A4
Brinton Cl DY11	12 C1
Brinton Cres DY11	12 C1
Broad St DY10	7 E3
Broadwaters Dr DY10	7 G2
Bromsgrove St DY10	3 E2
Bronte Dr DY10	8 A5
Brook St DY11	3 A2
Brookdale DY10	7 F2
Brooklands Dr DY11	7 E1
Brookside Way DY10	9 F1
Broom Cres DY10	7 H5
Broomfield Cl DY11	6 C3
Broomfield Green DY11	3 A1
Broomfield Rd DY11	3 A1
Brown Westhead Park DY10	5 E5
Browning Cl DY10	7 H5
Bruce Rd DY10	7 H3
Bull Ring DY10	3 D2
Burghley Dr DY11	3 A2
Burlington Cl DY10	7 H6
Burns Cl DY10	7 H4
*Butcher Green, Claines Cres DY10	7 H5
Butts La DY10	17 F2
Byron Cl DY11	8 A6
Cairndhu Dr DY10	7 H3
Cakebole La DY10	17 G1
Caldwell Cres DY11	3 C3
Callows La DY10	3 D1
Canterbury Rd DY11	6 A3
Captains Pool Rd DY10	13 G3
Cardarin Av DY10	13 H1
Cardinal Dr DY10	13 H1
Carlton Cl DY11	6 B3
Carlyle Av DY10	7 H4
Carpet Trades Way DY11	3 C1
Carroll Walk DY10	8 A6
Carter Av DY11	3 A4
Castle Rd DY11	3 C3
Cathedral Av DY11	6 A4
Caunsall Rd DY11	5 G2
Cavendish Dr DY10	7 H3
Cedar Cres DY11	3 A1
Cedar Dr DY11	3 A1
Chaddesley Gdns DY10	7 G5
Chaddesley Rd DY10	7 G5
Chadwick La DY11	16 A4
Chaffinch Dr DY10	13 F3
Champney House DY10	13 F2
Chapel Ct DY10	7 H1
Chapel Hill DY11	7 G1
Chapel St DY11	3 C2
Charles Av DY10	7 G1
Charles St DY10	3 E2
Charlton La DY11	16 A1
Chatterton Walk DY10	8 A5
Chaucer Cres DY10	8 A5
Cherry Orchard DY11	3 F2
Cheshire Gro DY11	6 B4
Chester Rd North DY10	7 G2

18

Woodlands Cl DY11 16 B4
Woodlands Rd DY10 5 F4
Woodward Rd DY11 12 C1
Worcester Cross Ringway DY10 3 E1
Worcester Rd, Hartlebury DY11 16 B6
Worcester Rd, Kidderminster DY11 7 E6
Worcester St DY10 3 D2
Wordsworth Cres DY10 7 H4
Wrekin Cl DY11 12 C2

Yellowhammer Ct DY10 13 G3
Yeoman DY10 13 F2
Yew Tree Rd DY10 3 F3
York Pl DY10 7 E3
York St DY10 7 E3

STOURPORT-ON-SEVERN

Abberley Av DY13 15 A7
Almond Way DY13 14 B3
*Ankerdine Av, Langdale Way DY13 15 A7
Areley Cl DY13 15 B6
Areley La DY13 15 A5
Areley Common DY13 15 B8
Ash Gro DY13 14 C4
Aspen Walk DY13 14 B3

Bala Cl DY13 14 D3
Baldwin Rd DY13 14 E4
Barnfield Rd DY13 15 D7
Barracks Rd DY13 15 F7
Beach Rd DY13 15 B7
Bell Row DY13 15 D5
Berkeley Cres DY13 15 D7
Bewdley Rd DY13 14 C3
Bewdley Rd North DY13 14 B2
Bilberry Cl DY13 14 B3
Birchfields Dr DY13 14 B3
Bishop St DY13 14 D3
Bower Bank DY13 15 B6
Bower Hill Dr DY13 15 B6
Bowpatch Cl DY13 15 B7
Bowpatch Rd DY13 15 B7
Bredon Way DY13 15 A7
Briar Way DY13 14 B4
Bridge St DY13 15 C5
Brindley St DY13 14 C3
Broach Rd DY13 15 E7
Brocket Cl DY13 14 B2
Brockton Pl DY13 15 B7
Broomy Cl DY13 14 A3
Brunel Cl DY13 14 D3
Bullus Rd DY13 14 E3
Burlish Cl DY13 14 C2
Burlish Crossing DY13 14 B2
Buttermere Rd DY13 14 C2

Calder Rd DY13 14 B1
Callow Cl DY13 15 A7
Cedar Dr DY13 15 C6
Cedar Rise DY13 14 B4
Cheapside DY13 15 D6
Chequers Cl DY13 15 C7
Cherry Tree Walk DY13 15 B8
Chesshire Cl DY13 15 B8
Cheviot Cl DY13 15 A8
Chiltern Cl DY13 15 A8
Church Av DY13 14 E4
Church Dr DY13 14 E4
Church Walk DY13 15 B6
Claerwen Av DY13 14 B1

Cleeve Cl DY13 15 A8
Coniston Cres DY13 14 C2
Coopers La DY13 15 C5
Cotswold Av DY13 15 A7
Court Cl DY13 14 D4
Cranberry Dr DY13 14 B3
Cutty Sark Dr DY13 15 E6

Danescroft DY13 14 D4
Derwent Av DY13 14 D3
Dewberry Cl DY13 14 B4
Discovery Rd DY13 15 E6
Dorsett Rd DY13 14 D3
Dunley Gdns DY13 15 B6
Dunley Rd DY13 15 A7

East Rd DY13 14 E3
Easthope Cl DY13 15 C7
Elan Av DY13 14 B1
Elderberry Cl DY13 14 B4
Elm Gro DY13 15 B8
Elmfield Walk DY13 14 B4
Endeavor Pl DY13 15 E6
Engine La DY13 15 D5
Ennerdale Rd DY13 14 C2
Erneley Cl DY13 15 C6

Farm Rd DY13 14 E4
Ferndale Cl DY13 15 F5
Field End DY13 14 B4
Foundry St DY13 14 D4
Fowler Pl DY13 14 D3
Francis Rd DY13 14 B2

Galahad Way DY13 14 C4
Garland Rd DY13 14 B2
Gheluvelt Ct DY13 14 C4
Gibbons Cres DY13 14 D4
Gilgal DY13 14 E4
Golden Hind Dr DY13 15 E6
Grasmere Gro DY13 14 C3
Great Western Way DY13 14 D3

Hafren Way DY13 14 C4
Hanstone Rd DY13 15 C7
Hartlebury Rd DY13 15 E5
Hazeldene DY13 15 F5
Heathfield Rd DY13 15 F7
Heathlands DY13 15 F5
Heightington Pl DY13 15 B6
Hermitage Way DY13 15 C6
Hillside Cl DY13 15 B8
Hodfar Rd DY13 15 E7
Holly Rd DY13 14 E4

INDUSTRIAL & RETAIL:
Firs Industrial Est DY13 14 F1
*Riverside Business Pk, Hartlebury Rd DY13 15 E5
Sandy La Industrial Est DY13 15 E7

Jackson Cres DY13 15 C7

Katrine Rd DY13 14 C2
Kings Arms La DY13 15 B8
Kingsway DY13 14 B1
Kylemilne Way DY13 15 F5

Lane End Walk DY13 15 C7
Langdale Rd DY13 15 A7
Larford Walk DY13 15 C7
Layamon Walk DY13 15 C6
Lichfield St DY13 15 D5
Lickhill Rd DY13 14 C4
Lickhill Rd North DY13 14 A2
Lilac Gro DY13 14 C4

Lime Tree Walk DY13 14 B3
Linden Av DY13 15 B7
Lion Hill DY13 15 D5
Llangorse Cl DY13 14 B1
Llewellyn Cl DY13 15 F8
Lodge Rd DY13 15 D5
Lombard St DY13 14 D4
Longboat La DY13 14 E4
Longmynd Way DY13 15 A7
Lorne St DY13 14 D3
Lower Lickhill Rd DY13 14 B3
Loweswater Rd DY13 14 B1

Malham Rd DY13 14 C1
Malvern Cl DY13 15 B7
Manor Cl DY13 14 E3
Manor Rd DY13 14 E3
Maple Cl DY13 14 B4
Marlbourgh Dr DY13 15 C8
Mart La DY13 15 D5
Martins Way DY13 15 C5
Martley Rd DY13 15 B7
Mayberry Cl DY13 14 B4
Mayflower Cl DY13 15 E6
Meadow Vw DY13 15 B8
Mentieth Cl DY13 14 B1
Milford Av DY13 14 B2
Mill Cl DY13 14 F4
Mill La DY13 14 F4
Mill Rd DY13 14 E4
Minster Rd DY13 14 D4
Mitton Cl DY13 14 D4
Mitton Gdns DY13 14 D4
Mitton St DY13 15 D5
Mitton Walk DY13 15 D5
Moffit Way DY13 14 C4
Moor Hall Dr DY13 14 C4
Moorhall La DY13 15 C5
Mostyn Rd DY13 14 B2

Nelson Rd DY13 15 E7
New St DY13 15 C5
Nina Cl DY13 15 E5
North Rd DY13 14 E3

Oak Apple Cl DY13 15 B8
Oakdene DY13 15 F5
Oakhampton Rd DY13 15 B8
Old Ford Walk DY13 15 C8
Old Station Ct DY13 14 E4
Oldington La DY13 14 F1
Olive Gro DY13 14 C4
Olympus Gdns DY13 15 F5
Orchard Cl DY13 14 F4

Park Av DY13 14 C4
Park Cres DY13 14 C3
Parker Pl DY13 14 F1
Parkes Pass DY13 15 D5
Parkes Quay DY13 15 D5
Pearl La DY13 15 A7
Pembroke Way DY13 14 B2
Pine Walk DY13 14 B4
Pinedene DY13 15 F5
Pinta Dr DY13 15 E5
Power Station Rd DY13 15 E6
Prince Rupert Rd DY13 15 B6
Princess Way DY13 15 B7
Prospect Rd DY13 14 D4
Pullman Cl DY13 14 E4

Queens Rd DY13 15 C7

Rannoch Cl DY13 14 B1
Raven St DY13 15 C5
Rectory La DY13 15 A6
Redhouse Rd DY13 15 A8

Redstone La DY13 15 B8
Resolution Way DY13 15 E6
Ribbesford Dr DY13 14 B4
Ribbesford Rd DY13 15 A6
Ricketts Cl DY13 14 F1
Rose Dene DY13 14 B4
Rydal Cl DY13 14 C2
Ryvere Cl DY13 15 C6

St Bartholomews Rd DY13 15 B6
St Davids Cl DY13 14 B2
St Johns Rd DY13 14 E3
St Micheals Cl DY13 14 D4
Sandy La DY13 15 E7
Santa Maria Way DY13 15 E5
Sarah Seagar Cl DY13 14 B2
Saxiby Pl DY13 14 E4
Seedgreen Cl DY13 15 C7
Seven Hills Dr DY13 15 A8
Severn Rd DY13 15 D5
Severn Side DY13 15 D5
Sion Gdns DY13 15 D5
Snowberry Cl DY13 14 B4
Stagborough Way DY13 14 B4
Steatite Way DY13 14 B3
Stour La DY13 15 E5
Summer Cft DY13 15 B8
Summerfield Rd DY13 14 E4
Swiss Heights DY13 15 B7

Tan La DY13 14 D4
Tenby Way DY13 14 B3
The Birches DY13 15 F5
The Grove DY13 15 F5
The Hollies DY13 14 B2
The Priory DY13 14 D3
The Ridgeway DY13 14 C3
The Rough DY13 15 C6
Thirlmere Rd DY13 14 C2
Timber La DY13 14 F4
Torridon Cl DY13 14 B1
Trevithick Cl DY13 14 D4

Ullswater Av DY13 14 C2

Vale Rd DY13 14 D4
Vawdrey Cl DY13 15 B7
Vernon Rd DY13 14 D4
Victory Cl DY13 15 E6

Walton Cl DY13 15 B7
Ward Rd DY13 15 C7
Warwick St DY13 14 D3
Watery La DY13 15 E7
Watt Ct DY13 14 D3
Wenlock Way DY13 15 B7
Wesley Av DY13 15 C7
Wilden Top Rd DY13 14 F4
William Bullock Cl DY13 15 C5
William Coley Pl DY13 15 D7
Willowdene DY13 15 F5
Windermere Way DY13 14 B2
Windmill Cl DY13 15 C7
Windsor Dr DY13 15 C8
Witley Way DY13 15 B8
Woodbury Rd DY13 14 C3
Woodbury Rd North DY13 14 C3
Woodbury Rd West DY13 14 C3
Woodhampton Cl DY13 15 C8
Worcester Rd DY13 15 E5
Worth Cres DY13 14 B3
Wrekin Walk DY13 15 B7

Yarranton Cl DY13 15 B7
Yew Tree Walk DY13 14 B4
York St DY13 15 D5